SCHOOLMARMS
By Helen Guyton Rees

Ada Bell was a shy 16-year-old when she finished the grade school books at Boyd, Oregon and took a teacher's examination in The Dalles, then left for Bakeoven, Oregon "to begin my career" as she confided to her diary. In winter weather the horse-drawn stage bumped over rocky dirt roads, chilling and frightening her throughout the long day on the 40-mile trip. "And 40 miles was a long way in those days," she said.

She had only $4 to pay her fare, and no one was there to meet her when she alighted from the coach. With no money, where would she stay the night? She was troubled about the language barriers in the German-Swiss community, fearful of what the large students might do or say the first day at school, and determined to help them learn at any cost.

As she studied nights to keep up with her high school class, her great solace was (and the reader's delight will be) in reading letters from other child-teacher-friends about their teaching experience in different rural schools.

Ada's painful but exciting graduation from The Dalles High School recalls the 1901 school scene in that pioneer city.

Clever sketches by Elizabeth Rocchia, a Portland artist, enliven the pages of first-hand experiences Ada recorded in diaries, themes, and poems.

"I took my books and flowers from graduation down to the studio and had my picture taken."

"Schoolmarms"

By
Helen Guyton Rees

Binford & Mort
Publishing

2536 S.E. Eleventh • Portland, Oregon 97202

DEDICATION

Dedicated to my mother Ada Bell Guyton who never lost her youthful ideals and who throughout her life remained an inspiration to all who knew her.

APPRECIATION

Schoolmarms was published in *Oregon Education Journal* in three parts beginning January 1979, while Mary Don was editor of that monthly paper. Illustrations were done by the Portland artist, Elizabeth Rocchia. The author wishes to express appreciation for permission by O.E.A. Journal to use Ms Rocchia's whimsical drawings in the book *Schoolmarms*.

Thank you Doris Sias and Mary Morgan for the early reading of the manuscript and giving support and encouragement. The picture-copying talent of our niece Mary Ada Rose, as well as her constant involvement with details of writing, made sharing the work an expression of our common love for Ada Bell Guyton, her grandmother and my mother.

HGR

"*Schoolmarms*"
Copyright © 1983 by Helen Guyton Rees
All rights reserved. No part of this book may be reproduced in any form or by any electronic or mechnical means including information storage and retrieval systems without permission in writing from the publisher, except by a reviewer who may quote brief passages in a review.
Printed in the United States of America
Library of Congress Catalog Card Number: 83-73080
ISBN: 0-8323-0423-9
First Edition 1983

INTRODUCTION

Genealogy is an amazing hobby. It leads one from exciting discoveries to astonishing conclusions—often seemingly remote from the object of the search. For instance: what would ever lead one to read about the terrible cholera epidemics in Missouri in the early 1800's, except the search for an ancestor who lived (and died) in Missouri at that time?

Or why would one read of the migrations of the Algonquin tribes, except to find the truth of a family tradition claiming Pocahontas as an ancestor?

My mother, Ada Bell was from a family with such a story. This search of mine led me eventually to my own attic to open a box of letters tied up by my mother years before her death in 1958.

"There just might be something of interest about the family in these letters," I thought. As I read them, I realized I was finding Ada Bell, a bashful, timid girl of 16 "beginning her career," as she called it, teaching in outlying communities for a term or two, then returning to her high school classes in The Dalles.

Here I also found the "keepings of the years." A theme from English class, pressed flowers from the hills of Bakeoven—78 years old but still reminiscent of the eager, joyous search for beauty and achievement that was part of the life of Ada Bell. There were poems, pictures apparently drawn by students, scrapbook clippings, a "memory book" with tart or pithy sayings of classmates and friends, and a book with locks of hair more durable than the people from whose heads they had been clipped.

High ideals were expressed on every page; the desire to inspire, to encourage, and to help friends and students learn all that was possible during the short time they were in school. These child-teachers communicated attitudes, hopes, and intentions that beckon to teachers today. The writing styles were flowery and dramatic, according to the

I found the "keepings of the years"; A theme from English class, pressed flowers from the hills around Bakeoven 78 years old, a reminder of Ada's search for beauty, poems, pictures, a memory book. . . .

mode of the day. There was room for decorous fun, but through it all, life was a serious matter, and conscience was their guide.

CONTENTS

Chapter 1 "Career Begins"
Chapter 2 Letters
Chapter 3 High School Days

"Schoolmarms"

Chapter 1

"Career Begins"

Ada Bell was born in "Old Wasco County," now part of Idaho, in 1880 of parents, caught up in the poverty of the times, hoping to find security in one pioneer community after another. The frequent moves, the loss of three homes by fire, the family of eight children, all left their mark on Ada. She wrote in her "Story of my Life":

"I was bashful all of my childhood and found it difficult to talk to people even after I was grown.

"I do not remember learning to read, though I do remember spelling off the wallpaper (we papered our kitchens with newspapers, then), 'C-H-R-I-S-T-I-A-N E-V-A-N-G-E-L-I-S-T.' Mother was so surprised. I had never gone to school, and she didn't know I knew my letters.

"The first story I ever read was in the Youth's Companion. I wanted Mama to read the story on 'Children's Page,' and Irene or Leslie, one, said, 'Why, Ada, you can read that yourself,' so I did.

"I remember the first time I read in the Bible, it was the first chapter of St. John. I read it, 'In the beginning was the Word, and the Word was 'with good,' instead of 'with God.'" Irene told me about God.

"After knowing about God, I began to not be so much afraid. I knew He was looking after me, and wouldn't really let anything too bad happen to me.

"One day, I had a direct answer to prayer. I was still quite small, I think about eight. I seemed to be in the field, watching the horses or cows away from a haystack. And I had a rope. Then at once the rope was gone. I hunted and hunted and couldn't find it and I just knew Papa would be cross and maybe whip me. So down on my knees I got and asked God to help me find that rope. When I got up, I looked around, and on the side of a little knoll was the rope. You people who read this may laugh about it—of course the rope was there all of the time—but who can say that the Lord who watches after the sparrow didn't hear my prayer and answer it. He would surely listen to 'one of His little ones in distress.' And the memory has always been too sacred for me to talk about, and I even hesitated to write it now.

"I think I was about 12 or 13 when I joined the United Brethren Church. My sister Irene, brother Leslie and I were baptized in '15-Mile Creek' at the old Absolem Bolton place. There were many baptizings in that creek. Christianity has been the center of my life, the one thing around which all else revolves."

Teaching Backoven School at 16

"I was a little past 16 in February 1897 when Leslie and I went to The Dalles and took the teacher's examination. There were 23 who took it and Leslie and I were among the eight that passed. In March of that year, I began teaching at Bake Oven (original spelling), 40 miles away; and 40 miles was a long way in those days. I went on the stage from Boyd. It took all day. This was the first time I ever saw the Deschutes River which we crossed at Sherar's Bridge."

Bake Oven had a colorful beginning. In 1862 thousands of miners were rushing to the Canyon City Gold Strike 190 miles east of The Dalles. Pack trains headed across the deep canyons to the high desert country carrying needed supplies. According to the story, an enterprising French trader started from The Dalles with a pack train of flour. After he crossed the Deschutes River the first water to be found was in a canyon now known as Bakeoven. During

I began teaching at Bakeoven 40 miles away from home, and 40 miles was a long way in those days; it took all day.

the night Indians drove off his horses leaving him stranded with his supply of flour. While waiting to secure horses so he could proceed, he hollowed out a cave in the bank, built a crude oven, and baked bread which he sold to prospectors on their way to the mines. Eventually he bought horses and went on to Canyon City.

By 1897 Bakeoven was a stage stop with hotel, blacksmith shop, store, post office, school and meeting hall. It was surrounded by a growing farm community of mostly German and Swiss homesteaders and sheepmen who wanted their children to go to school and become Americans.

Schoolhouses in rural communities were usually crude, uncomfortable, sometimes dirty, and usually cold. The elevation at Bakeoven was around 3,000 feet where the winds blew off snowcapped Mt. Hood and below-freezing nights could be expected nearly six months of the year. Below-zero weather was common in winter storms. Terms of school were usually three months; if the money held out; or the teacher didn't quit, or get fired; or if the children didn't have to miss school to help with farming or take care of younger children (of which there were often many).

"I had only enough money to buy my ticket, I think Leslie let me have it, $4. I expected someone to meet me at Bake Oven. It was Saturday night, and supper time when we got there. No one was there to meet me.

"I was so frightened. The stage driver kindly offered to lend me the money for my night's lodging, but I said, 'No.' I'd have to ask Mrs. Burgess to trust me; but I had to do a lot of 'screwing' to get my courage screwed up to the asking point. I don't know what Mrs. Burgess must have thought of a teacher starting out without any money at all, but she was very kind, and put me at my ease.

"The next afternoon Mrs. William Kelsay came for me, and I boarded with her. I had, I think, seven pupils: Rosa, Ernest, Julia, and Anna Wakerlig and Leo and Jesse Fleming and Martha Borstel. I've realized for a long time that I was altogether too young to start out teaching, even though I could pass a teacher's examination. But I went back the next term, and the next until I taught there five terms [of three months each].

"The fall after I first taught, Inez Woolery and I batched in a house owned by her father, and went to high school in The Dalles. I went about two months when I had something like typhoid fever, and had to quit school. A year from the next January I went back, stayed at my sister Irene's this time. I took mid-year exam and passed, to my very great surprise, and went into the 9th A class. Of course, I didn't have money to go to school right along, so I would teach in the spring and fall and study to keep up with my class. I went to school in the winter."

Following is a theme written by Ada during her high school days.

My Career Began

"In April 1897, in all the beauty of springtime, my career began; that day to which I had looked forward with eagerness ever since my earliest childhood; that day for which I had longed, and planned, and dreamed. When I awoke that morning I wondered if it could really be true, or was it only a dream from which I would awaken, to find myself in the home I had left only two days ago.

"As I began my preparations for the day a feeling of dread took possession of me and I began to have a dim idea that I was incapable of doing that which I was about to undertake. I wondered what my school would be like. I had heard stories of pupils shutting the teacher out of the schoolroom. In these stories the teacher had generally gained the victory, either by physical strength or cunning, but I knew I should not be able to exercise either of those capabilities. I fancied if I should find myself locked out, I'd feel more like crying than fighting. Then I remembered reading about tricks played on the timid schoolma'am and shuddered to think of the effect should I open my desk and find a snake or lizard.

"I had heard of pupils who had refused to obey. Suppose some one of my students should say, 'I won't do it' in answer to my instruction. What would I do? When I had talked of being a schoolteacher, Father had tried to discourage me, by showing me that it would not all be smooth sailing, but I had not heeded his council, for was it not better to look on the bright side? And then, men didn't always understand. Now I almost wished I had heeded his words, and remained at home.

"My thoughts were here interrupted by the call to breakfast, so, trying to put on a calm, dignified air, I descended the stairs and entered the dining room.

"How unnatural it seemed to be in a new place where there was not one familiar face, and no one to understand my feelings, no one to give me a word of real friendly encouragement. Of course, it would never do to give in to such thoughts, so I made a doleful attempt to appear cheerful. I started to school early that morning, and after a few minutes' walk, stood at the door of my little schoolhouse.

"I remember thinking it strange that the door should be wired shut, instead of locked, but supposed the lock to have been broken. It was but the work of a moment to unfasten it and then the door swung open, and for the first time I beheld the room in which I was to spend many days.

"I cannot say that the sight of it was such as to revive my drooping spirits. I was accustomed to a country school, but nothing like this. And then I remembered the delightful schoolroom which fancy had portrayed as the one in which I should reign. I had never once imagined myself teaching in a room like this one. Large rude desks, floor of rough wood, walls also of rough lumber, no paper, no ceiling, not one thing to brighten the dull effect, only three windows and they were but half windows, bits of chalk and paper scattered here and there, while dust reigned supremely over all—this was the sight that met my

I remember thinking it strange that the door should be wired shut. I unfastened it and the door swung open. There were large rude desks, floor of rough wood, no ceiling, and bits of chalk and paper scattered here and there.

gaze, and my heart grew heavier, as I thought of spending three long months in that room.

"But I noticed with satisfaction that the desks were four in number, so I would probably have but a few pupils.

"However, there was no time to lose, so I diligently began my housecleaning, and by the time I had finished this, it was nearly nine o'clock. Looking from the window I could see the children coming up the path. I counted them, seven in all. As they came nearer, my heart seemed trying to jump out of my throat. I began to wonder what I should say to them. I supposed it was the proper thing to say, 'Good Morning' to each. I had heard other teachers do so. And I remembered some of my teachers and how kind they had been, really seeming interested in everything concerning me. By this time the children had almost reached the house, and, of course, it would never do for them to come in and find me staring out the window, so I hastily seated myself at my table, tried to put on an expression which would do credit to a teacher of years' experience, and waited.

"In that moment I think I understood something of what Joan of Arc must have felt while waiting for the kindling of the fire which was to usher her into the unknown world.

"But all things must end, and so, by the time my courage had all but vanished and my heart was beating as fast as it could beat, the time of suspense came to an end, and two children, a boy and a girl, entered the room and stood before me. I never before had known my tongue to come so nearly refusing to speak as it did that morning. By a powerful effort, I finally managed to articulate a faint 'good morning.' That broke the spell and I felt my scattered senses returning, and was now able to observe my new pupils. I thought from the looks of these two, that they had somewhat stubborn dispositions, and if their anger should be aroused, scolding or punishment would have little effect.

"The next to enter was a little freckled-faced German girl, very smart looking; followed closely by two other girls, one pretty, the other of a timid disposition. The last were two small boys, one with a mischievous sparkle in his bright eyes, the other looked like one who thought himself of much importance.

"These pupils constituted my school the first day, though there were others afterward.

"I had spoken as each one entered, and with every 'good morning' uttered I had gained new strength and courage, so that, by the time the hour hand of the clock pointed to nine, I felt capable of doing almost anything, and as I called school, I thought of my foolish misgivings of the morning.

"It did not take long to get my pupils to work, and then, while waiting for them to learn the lessons assigned, I had a short time to think.

"It is true my air castles had fallen, but I was learning a much-needed lesson, and though it caused pain for a short time, I saw that it was best to be content. These pupils were not the ones of whom I had fondly dreamed, but they were humans with intelligent minds, and were placed in my charge. I thought of how much I should try to do all I could to improve their minds, and how I'd try to help them to learn and be happy.

"The room, now that it contained bright-faced children, no longer seemed gloomy, and I wondered if it ever could seem so again.

"There was not a sound in the room save the 'tick-tock' of the clock, and being young in experience, I fondly imagined that it would continue so throughout the term."

POEM

Silently, on my little stand
Are some flowers in a can.
Roses red and bluebells sweet
Make our schoolroom quite complete.

Near the can is a little clock
Its quiet song, "Tick-tock, tick-tock"
Always tells us when it's time
To lay aside our books and dine.

Silently on my little stand are some flowers in a can. Near the can a little clock.

Excerpts From The Diary of Ada Bell Begun in 1900, kept until 1950

"SEPTEMBER 7, 1900: *I'm back to teach at Bake Oven—staying at Alden's. New students: Rosa Hauser and her brother Solomon, Rosa Borstel and Minnie Wakerlig.*

"*Rosa Hauser is a very sweet little girl; eyes are dark and they are always sparkling, her face is round with the sweetest dimple on each cheek. She seems to be smiling all the time. Her hair is short and her mother curls it. Solomon is a droll little fellow. One day they were late and I asked, 'You didn't stop to play did you?' and he answered, 'No Sir-ree!'*

"MONDAY 17: Bertha and Rosa Wakerlig and Julia McKinley came today. I now have three Rosas and two Julias. Mrs. Hauser was up yesterday afternoon so I came right home after school so I'd get to see her. I like her very much and she seems so affectionate.

"SEPTEMBER 29: Visit to Borstels: I like one of the German ladies very much, Mrs. Patjens, she looks so pleasant and good natured and kind. They talked German all the time, never speaking English except when addressing me and that was seldom. Of course, I've been there so much Mrs. Borstel thought I ought to feel at home, and so I did, but I wasn't going to put in my say when they were all talking—they could all speak English almost as well as I, but then I guess they'd rather talk their own language. I felt all right about it by the time I reached home and I told Mrs. Alden about it and we had a good laugh together. Mrs. Alden and I laugh about all the time.

"We had examinations last week—a very busy time for me. I'm sure I felt worse about each low mark than the pupils did.

"OCTOBER 19: I'll try to spend five hours a day studying [high school subjects]. Bertha, Rosa, and Julia have left school so my school is getting nearer to its usual size. I played 'I spy' with the children at noon.

"THE WAY I SPENT ONE AFTERNOON AT BAKE OVEN SCHOOL"

"SATURDAY, OCTOBER 20, 1900: This morning I studied 'till noon, went to the schoolhouse, built a fire, put some water on the stove, and while it was heating, outlined some Civil Government. Then I washed the windows, my table, the desks and scrubbed the floor. I think it will make all the next week better, for who cannot do better in a fresh, clean house? I went home with Jessie Friday.

"TUESDAY, NOVEMBER 6: Three students.

I'll try to spend five hours a day studying. This morning I studied 'till noon.

"WEDNESDAY, NOVEMBER 7: Five.

"THURSDAY, NOVEMBER 8: Five pupils. We were to have had Church at the 'Palace of Babel' last Sunday [a dance hall over the blacksmith shop] but Mrs. Hauser didn't get word in time to come so we all went down there. Mrs. Alden rode in the hack with Borstels and Martha and Helen rode in the wagon with us. There were about 20 there, counting children. He is a German preacher but preached in English and read the Bible in both English and German. He preached a sermon in German about the 'Nobleman's Son' and in English about the 'Pearl of Great Price'—said some very good things.

"Mrs. Hauser wants me next Friday, and Mrs. Borstel a week from then. [Teachers lived with parents a week or two in each home.]

"NOVEMBER 9: Jessie, Solomon and Rosa—only three pupils today. This afternoon we had company—Miss Violet Melville and the Hinton children. I was real glad to have them come, but how I wished they had come on a day when I had all the pupils. I think they will come back the last day though.

"I got the Testaments in the mail today for my pupils. I hope they will read them.

"NOVEMBER 15: My pupils were a little wild this week. I suppose it is because school is so nearly out. I worried so much about it I had a headache. I thought for a long time about what I ought to do. I finally decided to take a whip to school. It worked like a charm. I never had a better school.

"NOVEMBER 21: Ice bound. No pupils since Monday. So cold I can't get home. Went home with Martha Friday evening and Monday I got so cold coming to school I took a very bad cold. Monday night the wind blew from the East and about two inches of snow fell. It was 7 above zero—it is a little warmer now, though.

"THURSDAY, NOVEMBER 22: Somewhat warmer, but looked like more snow—and IF it did, I couldn't get home at all, so we decided I might as well go home for we had no idea that the pupils would come back for Friday. After breakfast I went back to the school, burned the rest of the wood and papers 'In honor of McKindly,' I said [just elected president].

"Went home to Aldens' and worked on the register 'till one o'clock, then took myself to my 'Castle on the North Pole' to do my packing. Put on all the clothes I could get on so I wouldn't take cold.

"Loyal took me to Bake Oven. I just had time to catch the stage, about 7 when I got to Shaniko. Ate supper at the restaurant and then called on Jessie McLeod, then went to bed. Slept one good nap and then woke up and more sleep again was impossible for a long time. When I did doze off it was just to dream that I could hear people getting up and rushing off to meet the train. After breakfast I went to the depot. There were no seats in the depot and I got impatient and tired waiting. At Biggs we had to wait two hours for our train. Oh, how tired I did get!

"MARCH 11, 1901: Just received the verification of my being hired to teach again at Bake Oven.

"APRIL 15: Eight pupils: This afternoon Willie and I went on a tramp. We went to 'green gulch,' we called it, and followed it down to the canyon and then from there on home. Someone was at Hauser's sheep corral, but we kept our faces hid behind our big sunbonnets, for we were not attired for company. Yesterday four pupils.

"JUNE 28: Yesterday I picked raspberries for Mrs. Alden and this morning I picked peas. I wonder if I shall ever enjoy teaching another school as much as I have this.

"I have just returned from Hausers' where we went this afternoon. We walked and Mrs. Alden had a terrible time, going through sand banks and climbing over sagebrush and stubbing her toes on the rocks. I felt sorry for her. Willie led her part of the way, and I the rest. We had a very nice visit after we got there. [Mrs. Alden was losing her sight.]

"THURSDAY, JULY 4: My school closed yesterday afternoon. Mrs. Fleming, Leo, Jessie, Willie and Rosa came, and thinking no one else was coming, I commenced my program about 2:20. We had just finished and I commenced to make a few closing remarks when I heard a rap on the door. I opened it and found Mrs. Hauser and her two children there, so we just gave our program over again, as the children were all willing—then I told all my children goodbye and went home with Mrs. Fleming.

"The next day I went up to my schoolhouse for the last time—I believe it is the last time. I swept the schoolroom and took down the pictures; I wanted to bring them away with me.

"Before leaving I knelt down and prayed for my pupils and asked that I might be allowed to meet every one on the

It was 2:30, so supposing no one else was coming, the children went ahead with the program. Just as they were finishing Mrs. Patjens, Mrs. Borstel, and Mrs. Hinton came. I was so embarrassed. We gave the program again.

other shore. I shall always think lovingly of the place and people and my dear, dear pupils which almost seem to belong to me, I love them so.

"They will take me to Shaniko in the morning where I will take the train to The Dalles. I dread the long ride on the cars alone."

Farewell to Bakeoven

"When death's dark waters roll over me,
   when the light of my life is gone,
When my spirit has ascended to the Father's
   judgment throne,
When the earth is gay with flowers,
   and grass grows in the glen,
And the air is filled with songs of birds—
   who will miss me then?

When the earth is gay with flowers, and grass grows in the glen, and the air is filled with the songs of birds—who will miss me then?

*"The flowers will bloom their sweetest,
  the birds will sing as gay,
The grass will grow and the wind will blow,
  when my spirit is far away.
But O, could I only leave some sweet kind
  thought behind
That would make someone the better—
  that would make some heart more kind."*

(The conclusion to be written when the writer grows old.)

CONCLUSION
(Written in 1946—the writer WAS old.)

"The years have passed and now OLD am I,
So to finish this poem I'll certainly try.
Of such silly, dramatic, sorryful stuff,
You, reader of this, have had quite enough.

"Who would have thoght from a poem so gloom,
I'd still be living, and not in the tomb.
It sounds as if I were just pining away,
Broken-hearted and lonely, with no friends to stay.

"As a matter of fact, I had friends by the dozen.
My school days were happy, and life just a buzzin'.
When vacation time came, I went home to the folks.
There was fun and laughter and teasing and jokes.

"I went back to teaching the very same school.
Friends are easily made, if you follow this rule.
'To have friends you must be simply a friend.'
I've found this true from beginning to end."

Ada Bell Guyton

Chapter 2

Letters

Letters from turn-of-the-century teachers to their classmate Ada Bell.

"The Dalles, Oregon
June, 1900

"Dear Ada:
... "I was delighted to hear of all your plans in the school work. I am afraid mine will not be of much interest to you, but still I agree with you in the helpfulness of teachers being co-workers.

"Although my school is very small, there being only seven, my time is well employed. I hear 15 classes. I have four in my primary class, and it is the teaching of these little ones that I enjoy the most. It is this class I see so progressive in advancement.

"I have two third-grade pupils. The most advanced pupil is in the sixth grade, or rather, as nearly as he can be graded at all, for you know how it is in the country school.

"I use the phonic method a great deal in my primary spelling, and it is surprising the new words they master using it. I feel quite proud of this little class, as their slates are seldom without a hundred.

"I feel some discouragement about the entertainment I hoped to give for the benefit of a library. I feel doubtful concerning the success in a financial point of view, but still I may make a beginning which will be a little help. As the district is small they will not expect a great deal. It makes *it quite hard as there are but few young people about here, and they are quite indispensible to a successful entertainment.*

Your Friend, Martha Baldwin"

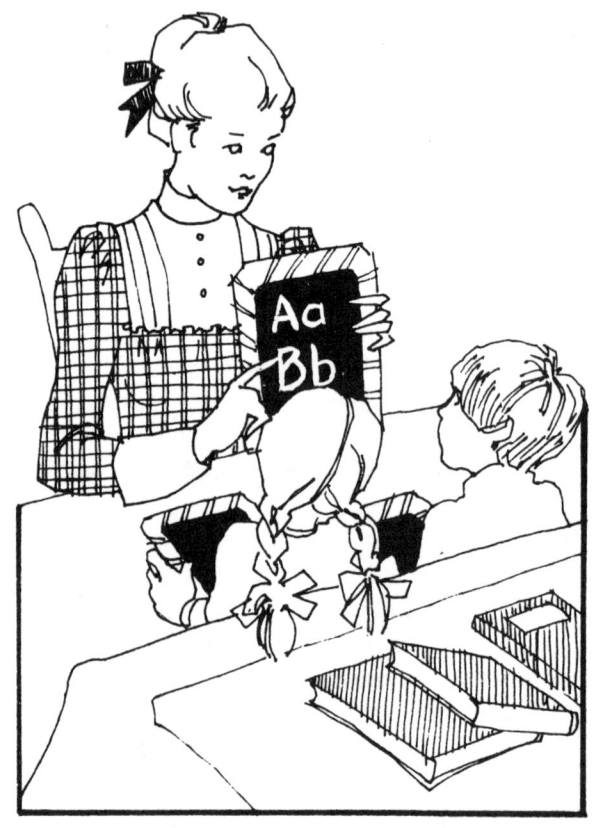

I have four in my primary class, and it is the teaching of these little ones that I enjoy most.

[No heading]

"Dear Ada:

[This year] "I have an enrollment of thirty-two pupils, with an average daily attendance of twenty-eight, so you may see I have no idle moments. I have all the grades from

the first to the eighth inclusive with the exception of the third. I also have a class of five little beginners which are very interesting little workers, and I only wish I might have a little more time to devote to them. I try to give them plenty of busy work to keep them out of mischief when I am so busy with the older ones.

Martha Baldwin"

Dear Ada: I have an enrollment of thirty-two pupils, with an average daily attendance of twenty-eight, with all grades first to eight except third; so you see I have no idle moments.

[Among the classmates who corresponded fairly regularly, Stella has to be the wittiest and most interesting.]

"April 23, 1900

"Dear Ada:

"You are now, I suppose, a teacher at Bake Oven. Was the examination hard, and what was your average?

"You have, perhaps heard of my sudden departure for out here on Five Mile. Wrote the letter Saturday morning, went out Saturday evening.

"I now have fourteen pupils enrolled, but the first week I had an average daily attendance, two. You can imagine how exciting it was. I am enjoying teaching ever so much more this Spring than I did last Fall.

"I have a very nice place to board, only one child in the family, a boy of sixteen who isn't attending school.

"Three new boys started school this week. The oldest is twelve, the youngest eight, and they had never attended school before. One of them can say his letters but does not know how they look, so you can imagine the fine time I will have with them.

"One of my boys, the youngest I think, is just as cute as he can be. Says some of the funniest things and I laugh at him. Ada, I was never cut out for a teacher, I laugh at all the silly things.

Stella"

"June 14, 1900

"Dear Ada:

"Only tomorrow and next week. HURRAH!!!! And then I will be done teaching children more than I know myself.

"Your experience of scrubbing the floor reminds me of myself. I carried three buckets of water up the hill and scrubbed out the schoolhouse and nearly killed one of the world's brightest STARS. Ha, ha.

"No. I have no opening exercises as I cannot sing—and I did not know that reading the Bible was allowed in Oregon. The Catholics made so much fuss in Nebraska that they had to stop it. It's late now, I must close, yours as ever,

Stella"

"Five Mile
September 27, 1900

"Dear Ada:

"I am now out here again and must say I like it better than a new school. I am enjoying it all. You did not say anything about keeping up with your studies. I am trying hard to keep up in Algebra, Geology, English Literature and American History. I have given up trying to graduate. Mr. Landers says it is next to impossible and do myself justice, so I have decided to go ahead and learn all I can just to know it and not for the sole purpose of graduating.

"Your Dutch and Swiss children remind me that perhaps I may have some half-breed Indians soon, all the rest are purely American, and good hardy ones at that.

"I see you will not satisfy my curiosity concerning that buggy ride, but very well, I will not tell you about something I know.

"I guess Amanda B. is at the hop yards. The rest are all here. My good Ray and my funny Ray are going so I get along very well.

"Do you have three months out there? Are you coming back to school afterwards?

"Edna is enjoying her school fine. She has 54 pupils and so, of course, is kept busy.

"I must tell you one of the funny things that happened on Ona's school She said she put the word, 'mew' on the board. The children did not know what it was and she explained it quite fully and then asked for an animal that mewed. A little boy shouted out, 'a mule.' Of course she laughed. She seems to be having as much trouble as I am in keeping her face straight.

"One of my little boys, after having finished his work lay down in the seat to rest. As I was busy and he was quiet, I didn't say anything. All was quiet until a boy started to pass, then out went one bare foot and the other boy was smashed up against the wall. I wanted to laugh, but instead had to punish the little boy by sitting him in a corner.
Stella"

Ona wrote that she put the word "mew" on the board. After explaining the meaning she asked what animal mewed. A little boy shouted out, "A mule." Of course she laughed. She seems to be having as much trouble as I am keeping her face straight.

"February 2, 1901
"Dear Ada:
"One month of my new year gone. There has been considerable sleighing, but I didn't have a fellow so that didn't do me any good; also skating, but I didn't have my skates, so that didn't do me any good; also coasting and that did me worlds of good, as I had two good coasts (East and West). Isn't that very shocking for a schoolma'am?
Stella"

"The Dalles
March 27, 1901
"Dear Ada:
"Only two more days and another week is past. The first week of my second month. You wanted me to tell you all about my school so here goes.

"The schoolhouse is smaller than the one on Five Mile, in fact by measurement it is about 12 x 10 I think. It faces the south and is unfinished inside. Big cracks to let the air in, also two windows on each side. The blackboard is a tiny affair nailed on the wall, but has the virtue of being smooth.

"Through the efforts of my predecessors and my own efforts the walls are plentifully covered with pictures. There are six homemade seats with room enough for two to sit on each. They are movable so you can guess how nice and noisy they can be if they choose.

"There are now only seven children, the other little girl having quit because I was going to put her back from the Fourth Reader into the Third. She was not ready for the Fourth, hardly ready for the Third, but she brought the Fourth so I let her try it. She said, 'If I can't read in the Fourth, I won't read in any.' I said, 'You will probably do as I tell you if you come to school here.' She said, 'Then I shant come to school.' I was silent and she quit last Friday. The other children, however, are all obedient children.

"There are the three Stoneman children: two boys, Henry, age 10 and Herman, age 6, and Amelia, age 7. They are all fairly smart. I sometimes think too smart. For instance, the other day Henry raised his hand and, of course, I asked him what he wanted. He said, 'The bottom of my foot itches.' I looked at him for a moment or two in complete astonishment, then said, 'Well, I have no intention of scratching it,' and then I gave him a good talking to and since then he hasn't been quite so foolish.

"The Stoneman children all are fair and blue-eyed. Herman is a funny little chap; is rather pretty. The other day I said to him (he was teasing one of the little girls), 'Little boys shouldn't tease little girls.' He said, 'Well, my Papa does my Mama and this morning he made her cry.' I felt queer to say the least.

Stella"

[No date given]

"Dear Ada:

"Did you ever attempt to make your boys polite? My little Swede boy got mad at one of the little girls who accidentally hit him. He was telling what he was going to do after school and I said, 'Emil, don't you know that gentlemen do not strike girls?' He looked at me a moment and then said, 'Then I'm not a gentlemen, because if she hits me, I'll hit her back.' Thus ended my first attempt to teach him to be polite.

"A few days later as the children were getting a drink, I attempted a second lesson. One little girl had been waiting a long time but she gave up the cup to him. 'Emil,' I said, 'Don't you know that it is polite to let a girl drink first?' He put the cup to his lips then looked over it in the most astonished way and said, 'No, is it?' and took his drink. Thus endeth the second lesson, and I haven't tried since.

"One of my classes had to write sentences from words in their readers and one of the words was 'sprung.' This is

what one little girl wrote, 'The dogs sprung their legs at the man.' How's that? It struck me rather funny.
                                                Stella Brown"

He looked at me a moment then said, "Then I'm not a gentlemen, because if she hits me, I'll hit her back." This ended my first attempt to teach him to be polite.

"Five Mile, Oregon
The Dalles
[No date]

"Dear Ada:

"I am 'Miss Brown' out here all the time. I hate it and spoke to Mrs. Runyan asking if they wouldn't call me 'Stella,' but she said her boy was losing all his manners and she didn't want him to get too fresh (at school)—so I am 'miss-ed' all the time.

I look a heap better than Maud Muller in my sunbonnet.

"I look a heap better than Maude Miller in my sunbonnet. There are two or three little 'kids' who go barefooted when it is warm enough.

"Those three boys who dropped out of school live such a terrible distance from the schoolhouse.

"Mr. Gilbert and Mr. Gifford were out last Wednesday and took pictures of the schoolhouse, schoolchildren and schoolmarm. I intend to have both preserved. Irene refused to have her picture taken. She is terribly bashful. There was only six had theirs taken, but my funny Ray and my good Ray were both there so I don't feel so bad about it.

Mr. Gilbert and Mr. Gifford were out and took pictures of the schoolhouse, schoolchildren, and the schoolmarm. Irene refused to have her picture taken. She is terribly bashful.

"I have had a new pupil start—he is almost 16 and every bit as tall as I am. He isn't very advanced. He thinks he is rather smart, but then he behaves himself fairly well so I let his smartness pass.

           Stella Brown"

[Not dated]
"Dear Ada:

"Your industrious studying shames me terribly for as usual I am awful lazy when my school duties are over for the day. I study American History after I get to school in the morning. After a few simple duties I have from half- to three-quarters of an hour for good hard study on it before the children come. I get home after school sometimes at half past four, sometimes at five. For a while I tried to study in the room where the rest of the folks were, but since I have really got to work, I study in my room. Ug, but it is cold, but I stick it out. Are you making outlines in any of your lessons?

"I am having a very small school this fall. Had twelve on the register who have started this term but have only eight now, and this week so far the attendance has been terrible. Monday no one came, Tuesday, two came, today two. Lively times, don't you think?

"I may have only two months here and then I may have more. It depends entirely on how much money they have. I have decided to teach next spring also.

"Edna has fifty-six pupils and says she is rushed all the time. All under fourteen too.

           Stella Brown"

"April 26, 1901
"Dear Ada:

"There is a row in the district. The clerk who hired me for some reason (because I am strict with his children, some people say) thinks he does not want me to teach another month, while the directors do want me. Which will come out first remains to be seen. My position is anything but enjoyable—between two fires.

Stella"

"Antelope, Oregon
[Not dated]

"Ada:

"I was so amused at some of the things you told me, I gave my intermediate pupils a test in Geography and Physiology. Oh, how I laughed over the papers; some of the answers were too dreadfully funny for any use. I feel as though I ought to tell you some of them. Well, here goes: You can guess the questions by the answers.

"'There are 8 ribs; the head is protected by the skull. The divisions of the upper limbs are the hip, thigh, leg and foot.'

"'The scapula is the name of the bone in the leg from the hip to the knee, it is the biggest bone in the body.'

"'There are three kinds of joints, the ball and socket, the hinge and the dove-tail. The ball and socket joint is in the elbow, the dove-tail joint is fastened to the fingers, and the hinge joint to the brain.'

"When I looked over the papers I could not help feeling bad for I had worked so hard with this pupil trying to get both Physiology and Geography into her head. I tell her something and in less than two minutes she cannot tell me what it was. It just worries me. Here are some of the answers she gave in Geography:

"'Cattle and horses is two of the principal products of New York.'

"'The south Atlantic States is New York, Maryland, Georgia, and Carolina and their climate is very high.'

"'We get cotton, rice, and sugar cane from Oregon and the climate is awful cold.'

"'New York excels in tobacco.'

"I could have cried when I looked over that paper.

"You asked me if I visited at the homes of my pupils, well rather, as only two families send to my school and I board around. I spent six weeks with one family and am now quartered in another house where I shall remain until I go home.

"I like it out here very much indeed, everyone is so kind to me.

"Where I am now, there are five small children and oh, they are so noisy that they almost drive me wild. I stay at the schoolhouse to do most of my writing because the noise bothers me so much.

"I feel perfectly at home here. I can go and come as I please. I help Mrs. Reese sometimes with the work and I like to help too. The other night we had some freighters here for supper. I helped her and made chocolate creams.
Ola"

"Antelope, Oregon
November 3, 1900
"Dear Ada:

"I am quite anxious to get a winter school and if you think it possible that they may have a winter school in your home district I should surely like to have it if I could.

"My school will be out the 30th of November. I like teaching so well that I feel as though I could go on teaching forever and ever. I have just written one of the directors in your home district, also to Mr. Underwood.
Ola Norman"

"The Dalles
June 18, 1901
"To the Right Honourable Miss Ada Bell who fills the exalted position of Chief Dish Washer at the Bell Farmhouse—
Greetings:

"Most honored Madam, it is with a quaking heart, an aching head and a torturing corn that I take up a scratchy pen and the poorest ink and attempt to chronicle the events that have transpired since last we met, for your amusement.

"Oh! For a sight of that face so fair
The eyes of blue and golden hair
That clusters in ringlets o'er thy marble brow,
What would I not give to see thee now.

"Could I but see thee, O love of mine!
I'd have many words for those eyes of thine
But as that privilege is not granted to me
I will have to write the words to thee.

"There, my inspiration is gone, but perhaps it is better for us all, for a little bit of a poem like this would go a long ways.

      Lots of love, from Ola Norman"

      "November 15, 1902
"Dear Ada:
"We have been having rain, rain, rain and RAIN! The roads are awful and the mud on the schoolroom floor!"
      [Unsigned—perhaps from Ola]

[Lillie McKeller taught at Bakeoven after Ada Bell graduated from high school.]

      "Bake Oven, Oregon
      May 26, 1901
"Dear Ada:
"I was quite surprised at the schoolhouse the morning I got here. This seemed such a dreary place when I first got here, but I wouldn't exchange for any other now. It was so dirty, the men had been there on Saturday and they worked in the house some. They built two new desks and patched up the walls and windows. The desks and seats almost filled the house, they have to be set cross-ways now in two rows. But I got it straightened out in a day or two and

moved the table over in the northeast corner, to make more room.

"Bertha Wakerlig met me at Shaniko and we ate supper there and started home about 7 o'clock. The hack had broken down when she was coming over and that had to be fixed.

"I think the road over there is about as rough as any I've ever seen. The wind was blowing that night and it was real cold and I got so sleepy.

"Mr. Burgess' folks had gone to bed and so Bertha took me over to her home and then we came over here the next morning. We got here about half after nine.

"The Mickle children and Borstels and Wakerlig children were there. Jesse came on Friday. I think a great deal of Solomon and Rosie. Isn't Rosie mischievous?

Lillie McKeller"

[Bessie Underhill apparently taught at Bakeoven after Lillie McKeller.]

"Bake Oven, Oregon
[Not dated]

"Dear Ada:

"You spoke of my plans for teaching, Ada. I think my plans are very much like yours, I want to get them as far along in their books as I can and to remember as much as possible by reviewing whenever I think it necessary. I am well pleased with the work my pupils have been doing during the three weeks time I have been here. Little Katie Borstel is very quick in her studies, and has never missed one day so far. Rosa [Wakerlig] came two weeks and I do not know whether she will come any more or not as her sister is not at home and it leaves so much work for her mother. I hope she will soon get started as I do not like to have my pupils absent one day as the term is short and

they have a poor chance so far away from school. There will be two months and perhaps three, I am not sure yet.
                    Bessie Underhill"

Poem written in 1900 after the children had gone home from school.

Bakeoven School

*In a green and pleasant hollow stands a schoolhouse
   all alone.
On the hills which quite surround it, tall and sweet
   the grass has grown.
Near, the pile of wood is lying like some strange
   fantastic thing.
Yet it warms the little schoolhouse when the wind blows
   cold in spring.
In this schoolhouse of rough lumber all is coarse
   and bare and old,
But the roof, so old and rusty, shelters hearts of
   brightest gold.*

*In the west wall is the blackboard. Here the children
   learn to write.
And their letters seem right awkward, 'till they've
   learned to make them right.
Near the blackboard stands the bucket, crayon box,
   and washing pans.
In this corner to the northwest is a stand with
   cloth of red.
There are clock and books and papers; near them bends
   the teacher's head.*

*In the east wall there are pictures drawn by little
   children's hand,
And they show some rare good talent, which may
   some day bless our land.*

"Where is Oregon, Lake Erie, Gulf of Mexico, and
   Hudson Bay?"
In the doorway stands the teacher. Sweet by chimes
   the little bell
And the children stand in line, learn to march in,
   straight and well.

First in line is Master Ernest, who will some day
   be a man.
But he knows the sweets of childhood; let him laugh,
   as boyhood can.
Then his little sister Anna, with her head of light
   brown hair,
And her face so round and rosy is a face of
   childhood fair.
Next in line their sister Julia who does make our
   school more bright,
With her laugh all soft and mellow and her eyes
   which sparkle bright.

Fourth in line is Helen Borstel with her sweet,
   good-natured way,
And a smile is on her countenance, and her face is
   bright each day.
Here is Jesse, little urchin, who has mischievous
   brown eyes,
That are always fairly dancing; still he looks so
   wondrous wise.
Now comes darling little Katie with her hair of
   brightest red,
And her face so round and pleasant, and a wise and
   knowing head.

Seventh in line is Lillie, who though sometimes
   is mad,
Yet an affectionate child she is, and a kind heart
   she has had.

*Eighth is Martha; oh, dear Martha, often noble, good
and kind,
With a heart of deepest virtue and a pure and
thoughtful mind.
Then in marches jolly Walter, last but ah, not least
is he.
His impish face is smiling and he laughs with
boyish glee.*

*"Stand in line, all ready, march" now the teacher's
voice is heard,
When the line moves in the building, to the answer
of her word.
This little schoolhouse long may stand, but the children
all will grow.
Others come to take their places; ones that we may
never know.
The sun will shine, the rain will fall, the grass will
grow as green;
Should the schoolhouse disappear, and the children
not be seen.*

Graduates

Chapter 3

High School Days

Ada Bell's account continues:

"The last year I attended high school the full nine months. I can never understand why I was so frightened and bashful when I first started high school. I could hardly answer when I was spoken to, and at first would lose my tongue when called on to recite, but we had monthly tests and so the teachers discovered that I wasn't so dumb as I acted. I usually had my problems all worked before class. Most of the kids would come to me for help with problems they couldn't get. I think that's how I got acquainted. I look back now on high school as the big thing in my life. It, and teaching, cured me of bashfulness and gave me self-confidence.

"I graduated June 1, 1901, then taught school at Summit Ridge, at Center Ridge two terms, then, and last, at Kent."

GRADUATION FROM THE DALLES HIGH SCHOOL (1901)
From Ada Bell's Diary

"WEDNESDAY EVENING, FEBRUARY 20, 1901: Dora Sexton and I went together to our first class meeting. It was at Rosemary Baldwins, and as she lives at the foot of the Rhinehart steps we went that way. I can't tell how many places we got into the mud, and how many 'rivers' and 'lakes' we had to jump over, and then the steps were fairly coated with ice, and altogether we had quite a time getting there. There was no one absent except Stella, and we are not sure of having her in our class. First, we elected officers: John Cooper, President; Joe Steers, V.P.; Bess Snipes, Secretary; and Rosemary B., Treasurer.

"After a little more so called 'business' we had chocolate and cake for refreshments, and then Pearl Grimes and Rosemary B furnished some music. John Cooper and Joe Steers were on their high horses. When we were partaking of our refreshments, John said, 'Where is Grace Davis?' and on being told that she is not a member of our class, he said, 'She makes Gooboo eyes at me,' and kept that going all the evening. At one time, he was sitting near the window, when he jumped up, saying that he would not sit there any more, for she was looking in at the window and making gooboo eyes at him. Once during the evening, he pulled my hair just a trifle, and I asked him if he wanted a lock of it.

"The next day at school, where there was a whole crowd of girls around me, he marched up and asked if I was ready to give him that lock of hair. You should have heard the girls laugh, and I'm afraid I'll never hear the last of it.

"The members of the class of 1901 are as follows:

John Cooper	Dora Sexton
Joe Steers	Hannah Schwabe
Porter Frizzel	Blanche Emerson
Volney Driver	Bernie Schooling
Bess Snipes	Pearl Grimes
Bess Eddon	Rosemary Baldwin
Bessie Vogt	Ada Bell
Ortha Waters	

"SUNDAY, FEBRUARY 24: I went down to Sunday School. Stella wasn't there but her sister, Gertrude, told me that Stella could not finish. Mr. Landers was in favor, but Miss Hill and Mr. Neff were opposed. I was indignant to think of it. I wonder if Miss Hill had such an easy time in

Once during the evening he pulled my hair just a trifle, and I asked him if he wanted a lock of it. The next day at school, when there was a whole crowd of girls around me, he marched up and asked if I was ready to give him that lock of hair. You should have heard the girls laugh, and I'm afraid I shall never hear the last of it.

getting her education that she doesn't have any sympathy for anyone else. And Stella has worked **so** hard.

"MONDAY, FEBRUARY 25: This morning I awoke almost dreading to go to school, and kept thinking about how much I should miss Stella, and I felt real lonely, all the way to school. When I got there, Ninon and I were standing at the window talking, when I saw someone who looked a great deal like Stella coming with Gertrude. I thought it couldn't be she, for her school was to commence today, but when she got nearer, I saw that it was truly she. I was **surprised**. She said that they had decided to postpone school for a week or two. I was so glad to have her back.

Gertrude told me Stella could not finish high school just as Ninion was standing at the window. Then I saw someone that looked like Stella—it truly was she.

"When I was on my way to school this afternoon, I met Stella with her books on her way home, and she said they had changed their minds again and she had to go this afternoon. I don't believe I ever did miss anyone before as I shall miss her, for we have been together almost constantly, and I don't see how I'm going to get along without Stella. I need her example to help me to be good. I do feel so dreadfully lonesome. I think I'll work on my composition, and that may help me not to think of it.

"SATURDAY, MARCH 9: I went to class meeting last night. John Cooper entertained the class. Miss Nan Cooper was there and she made the evening very pleasant. We didn't do much class business. Ethel Nottingham was there and she, Pearl, and Rosemary furnished us with music. Then John took us all through the hospital. We had cake and chocolate. Then we played 'ghost' for a while, and commenced charades when it was time to go home, and it was 12:20 when I got home.

"FRIDAY, MARCH 15: This has been one of my sleepy weeks. I've hardly been able to study at all, evenings, so I didn't get around to write any. We got our report cards, and I'm most ashamed of mine, though I really didn't expect more. It was all very good except the American History, and it was only 80. My average was 92 3/5. I've made up my mind to work harder, and I believe I can bring my work up if I work hard enough.

"My deportment was only 95. I was truly ashamed of that, and have turned over a new leaf. Claude Kelsay sits behind me, now, so I have to be good.

"Tonight Lillie McKeller and I stayed at the schoolhouse, and I helped her in writing an application for a school. She is going to take the examination in April. I hope she can get a school.

"THURSDAY, MARCH 28: I got 84 in Botany. Not very good, considering that I've been here all the term. We had Geometry today. Don't think I can get 100 on that, after all the trouble I took with it. Stayed there all noon. Then came home for dinner, and didn't go back. Don't know what Mr. Neff will say. He actually asked me today if I had any propositions copied in my desk. As if I would cheat! I don't believe anyone ever thought me dishonest before. It made me feel bad, but Mr. Neff is getting old and cranky, and I ought not care.

"English Lit. tomorrow. Don't believe I'll get as high in anything as I did last final, though. I've been here all the time this term, and ought to do lots better.

"WEDNESDAY, APRIL 3: This morning Mr. Landers announced the class roll of 1901, those who had everything clear, as follows:

Volney Driver   Dora Sexton
John Cooper   Rosemary Baldwin
Ortha Waters   Ada Bell
Bess Eddon

"If the rest make up the work in a week they may finish, but if not, they cannot.

"FRIDAY, APRIL 5: Lillie McKeller and I got excused at 1:15 this afternoon, and we went up to the East Hill Primary and visited both rooms up there. I was well pleased with the rapidity with which Miss Cheadle's pupils could add and subtract. They also read beautifully, put so much expression into it, I was surprised. I wish I could reach the results she has. Miss Roberts' room was also very interesting. Her pupils were writing compositions. I couldn't help but wonder how she ever got them to understand paragraphing. I had such a time with some of my pupils about that. Miss Roberts gave us lots of good information about methods, etc. She was awfully good to us. I noticed how polite her pupils were. When they marched in, Lillie and I stood near the door watching them. As each one passed us, they said, 'excuse me.' Then Miss Roberts, when talking with us, insisted on any pupil that wanted to ask anything to ask to be excused. I thought it a nice plan. When the First Reader class in Miss C.'s class recited, two pupils brought books to us without being told. They all seemed so anxious to do just what the teachers wanted them to.

"SATURDAY, APRIL 20: Our class has been having a time over our essays. Only four were willing to deliver theirs, and, of course, that would not make up a program. So Mr. Landers told us that all must speak, except those whom he might excuse. He then excused Rosemary, as she is to have the music, and Blanche and Bessie Vogt, as they are exceedingly timid.

"I was hoping that Mr. Landers would be my helper, but Miss Hill is to be. My, how blue I felt over it last night. I have about decided to write on an axiom, 'The Whole is Greater Than Any of its Parts.'

"Our class colors are two shades of pink. Our yell is:
"Rig-a-gig Rig-a-gig Re Ri Ro,
Out of the High School here we go,
Buddy-da Buddy-da Buddy-dy-da-doon,
We are the ---------- of n'oughty-one. [1901]

"FRIDAY, MAY 10: I had actually commenced on my essay and thought the battle half over, but alas, for the plans of mortals! On Monday when I started to school after noon, I met Mr. Proff. J.S. Landers. He stopped me, and inquired about my essay.

"When I told him my subject, he laughed at me. He wondered why in the world I chose such a subject, and I don't remember near all he said, but I felt awful blue. To think that I had to go to all the trouble and worry of getting another subject. I just went down into the basement and squalled.

"Then after school I stayed to talk with Miss Hill about another subject. Have now decided on, 'The Face is the Index of the Soul.' Have written it once, but O, how I dread the giving it.

"SUNDAY, MAY 19: My essay is finished and almost learned and I pretended to rehearse it yesterday. How I **dread** graduating.

"MONDAY, JUNE 3, 1901: I did it. The graduating is over with now, and I feel as though a great weight is lifted from my shoulders. I didn't write much about how I dreaded it, but as the time drew near, I became a very nervous girl, would cry over nothing at all.

"Friday morning Miss Hill told us to be at the Opera House at 7 p.m. to rehearse. In the afternoon I went with Mrs. Angell to watch the silk-worms. It was very interesting. They're not so much different from other worms. They weave a web all over themselves for I believe six days. In time they develop into moths which eat their way out, but when the silk is wanted, the case is baked and the threads of silk unwound. These threads are so small they can hardly be seen.

"We went down to the Opera House. Bessie Vogt and Rosemary Baldwin came and we waited and waited. I was tired and curled up on a large chair and went to sleep.

"At 8:30 Bessie V. woke me and we all went home. Ola phoned to Miss Hill and found that they had changed the appointment to the High School building, and had sent me word, but, of course, I didn't get the word, not being at home.

"I was blue over it all of the evening. Miss Hill said for me to be at the Opera House at 9:30 the next morning and she would then hear me rehearse. I didn't rest so calmly that night but slept late in the morning. I was there at 9:30, but no Miss Hill. I waited and in the meantime became more nervous than ever. At last she came, but by that time the tears were in my eyes and it was all I could do to keep them back. At last she got me to the stage, but seeing that I couldn't rehearse, she said the boys might practice their song first, so I skipped to the basement where I sat in a dark corner and had a good hard cry. I don't believe I ever cried so much in four months before, as in the last four.

"Then I went up and rehearsed, but it was very unsatisfactory. I think Miss Hill and Mr. Landers both understood for they didn't criticize, only to say, '**All right** Ada.' As I left I began to wonder if I should stay so nervous, for if so, I knew I wouldn't be able to deliver in the evening, and after all of my rehearsing and worrying and the Folks all coming in and everything it would be a disgrace to the school if I should break down or do some other horrid thing.

"I went up to say Hello to Stella, and she insisted on my staying for dinner. I did so, and then went down to the train to meet my sister, Irene. We went to May's where they ate dinner.

"Then I came to Mrs. Angells and began my preparations for the evening. I phoned Aunt Jane and she said all the Folks were in and I must come up. I thought Mamma ought to come down as I was so rushed for time, but that didn't suit, so I started up there and again began to cry because I didn't have more time and was tired and I didn't know what all, and again I wondered if I could possibly be able to give my essay.

"Ola fixed my hair and helped me to dress and then she and Clemmie Davis went with me. I still felt somewhat nervous. Soon we took our places on the stage, and by this time my heart was in a perfect flutter. I felt my eyes assuming proportions resembling saucers, and the blood seemed to be deserting my lips, leaving them parched. I looked down and on the front seat was Mrs. Baldwin, who smiled and nodded to me. That encouraged me somewhat. I tried to see how many familiar faces I could see, but they were few and I sat on the very end, and somewhat behind the piano, which made it worse for me. Now, as at first, I felt almost as though I had 'stage fever.' The orchestra began playing and I tried to compose myself and looked and tried to smile at my classmates, but it didn't seem to do much good.

"After the music ceased, it was quiet for a moment, and then Bess Snipes stepped forward and began her oration, but after a few sentences hesitated and seemed to have forgotten. My heart ached for her. But she soon went on and got through with the rest very nicely. . . .

"My turn was next and I stepped forward, how I hardly know. As I looked at the crowd I was possessed with a longing to make every word distinct to every one in the hall.

"With my resolution, all fear left me and I started in with a great deal of confidence, and really got through much better than when I had rehearsed. I was surprised at myself and was so carefree the rest of the evening. The burden seemed to have all rolled away. It was such a relief.

"The others gave theirs very nicely, and then Mr. Gavin, after a talk to our class presented the diplomas. Rosemary's name was first on the roll and mine second, but he skipped mine. I thought it was just through mistake and wondered what he would do when he got through and found that he had one left.

"But he also left out John Cooper 'till nearly the last. Then he called John out and gave him a lovely talk about his being a soldier boy, about resuming his studies, etc. I wondered then what could possibly be in connection with my name, but thought there was surely nothing.

"At last they were all given but one. Then he began to talk about a scholarship offered by Whitman College and made quite a nice talk about it, and said that my standing being the highest I was entitled to that scholarship. I was **surprised, dumbfounded!!!** I had never dreamed of such a thing.

"The boys sang their last song and congratulations were heaped upon us. There were several strangers congratulated me, and others I barely knew. Papa was too proud to say anything, Leslie said I had done better than he even hoped for, and Irene said she was proud of me. Of course there were lots of others that said nice things. It all seemed like a delightful dream to me. Monday I took my flowers and books to the photographic studio and had my picture taken.

"So ended my schooling. I didn't use my scholarship, for I had to teach a few years to have money to go on. After two years I met Will Guyton and married him. I never taught school again; and have not been sorry—just happy in our marriage. We raised two boys and two girls, **just right**."

At last they were all given but one. Then he began talking about a scholarship; then he said my standing being the highest, I was entitled to that scholarship. I was surprised, dumbfounded, I had never dreamed of such a thing.

QUOTATIONS FROM ADA BELL'S SCRAPBOOK

"OUR BEAUTIFUL LANGUAGE"
By Mrs. Alex Snyder

"A boy who swims may say he's swum, but milk is
  skimmed and seldom skum,
And nails you trim, they are not trum.
When words you speak, these words are spoken,
  but a nose is tweaked
And can't be twoken, and what you seek is
  seldom soken.

"If we forget, then we've forgotten, but things
  we wet are never wotten,
And houses let, cannot be lotten.
The goods one sells are always sold, but fears
  dispelled are not dispoled.
And what you smell is never smoled.

"When young, a top you oft saw spun, but did you
  see a grin e'er grun,
Or a potato nearly skun?"

RIDDLES

"What long name did one of the Pilgrims have?
                                        Miles."

"What famous book does the journey of the Colonists
suggest?
                            Pilgrim's Progress."

"Why should we think the first New England girls were
bicyclists?
            A number of spinning wheels were seen."

"How many peas are there in a pint?
                              One P."

"What shape is a kiss?
                    Eliptical (a lip tickle)."

"What does man love more than life,
Hate more than death or mortal strife;
That which contented men desire,
The poor have and the rich require;
The miser spends, the spendthrift saves
And all men carry to their graves?
                              Nothing."

"THE CANDID LOVER"
Author Unknown

"'O Maiden, do you twang the lyre?' asked he;
  she made reply:
'I do not twang, but I desire to plainly state
That I am great at making apple pie.'

"'O Maiden, do you warble sweetly?' asked he;
  she simply said:
'Nay not a warb, but I can neatly prepare a steak
And I can make fine doughnuts and good bread.'

"'In matters elocutionary, what gifts do you reveal?'
'I do not elocute; I'm very demure, you know;
I'm handy, tho, at getting up a meal.'

"'O Maiden, others may be clever, and others may
  be sweet
But will you be my own forever? 'Tis very fine
To be divine—but still a man must eat.'"

INDEX

A

Aldens, 10, 11, 12, 13, 14; Mrs., 46, 47
Angell, Mrs., 46, 47
Antelope, 31, 32

B

B, Amanda, 23
Bake Oven, 2, 3, 4, 10, 13, 14, 15, 22, 33, 34
Baldwin, Mrs., 47; Martha 20, 21; Rosemary, 39, 40, 43, 44, 45, 46, 48
Bell, Ada, Ded., App., Intro., 5, 10, 12, 19, 21, 22, 25, 32, 33, 39, 40, 44, 54, 55, 56
Bell Family, 32; Irene, 4; Leslie, 4, 48; Papa Josiah Dock, 2, 54; John Robertson, 54
Bolton, Absolom Place, 2
Borstel, Mrs., 14; Family, 11, 12, Children, 34; Helen, 12, 36; Katie, 34, 36; Martha, 4, 12, 13, 20, 21, 37; Rosa, 10
Boyd, 54, 56
Brown, Stella, 22, 23, 24, 25, 26, 27, 28, 30, 31, 40, 41, 42, 43, 47

C

Canyon City, 2, 4
Center Ridge, 39
Cooper, John, 40, 43, 44, 48; Miss Nan, 43

D

Davis, Clemmie, 47; Grace, 40
Deschutes River, 2
Don, Mary, Appreciation
Driver, Volney, 40, 44

E

Eagle Creek, Or., 54
Eddon, Bess, 40, 44
Edna, 23, 30
Emerson, Blanche, 40
Emil, 26

F

Five Mile, 22, 25, 28
Fleming, Mrs., 14; Jesse, 4, 13, 14, 34, 36; Leo, 14; Willie, 14
Frizzel, Porter, 40

G

Gavin, Mr., 48
Gertrude, 41, 42
Gifford, Mr., 29
Gilbert, Mr., 29
Golden, Colo., 54
Grimes, Pearl, 40, 43
Guyton, Ada Bell, 17; Will, 49, 55; Helen, 53-55

H

Hausers, 14; Mrs., 11, 12; Rosa, 10, 13; Solomon, 10, 13
Hill, Miss, 40, 46
Hinton, Mrs., 14; Hinton Children, 13

I

Irene, 29

J

Joan of Arc, 8

K

Kelsay, Mrs. William, 4; Claude, 43

L

Lake, Seth, 54; Hulbert, 54; Leonora Samantha Josephine, 54

Mc
McKeller, Lillie, 33, 34, 36, 43, 44
McKinley, Julia, 11
McKinley, Pres., 13
McLeod, Jessie, 13

M
Melville, Miss Violet, 13
Mickle Children, 34
Morgan, Mary, Appreciation
Muller, Maud, 28, 29

N
Neff, Mr., 40, 44
Norman, Ola, 32, 33
Nottingham, Ethel, 43

O
O.E.A. Journal, Appreciation
Ona, 23, 24

P - Q
Patjens, Mrs., 11, 15
Pike's Peak, 54

R
Ray, "Good" and "Funny," 23
Rees, Helen Guyton, 56
Reese, Mrs., 32
Rhinehart, (steps), 39
Roberts, Miss, 44
Rocchia, Appreciation
Rose, Mary Ada, Appreciation
Runyan, Mrs., 28

S
Schwabe, Hannah, 40
Schooling, Bernie, 40
Sexton, Dora, 39, 40, 46
Sherar's Bridge, 2
Sias, Doris, Appreciation
Shaniko, 15, 34
Snipes, Bess, 40, 47
Snyder, Mrs. Alex, 50
Steers, Joe, 40
Stoneman Children; Amelia, Henry, Herman, 26
Summit Ridge, 39

T
The Dalles, 2, 5, 15, 19, 32, 39, 55

U
Underhill, Bessie, 34, 35

V
Vogt, Bessie, 40, 45, 46; Blanche, 45

W
Wakerlig Children, 34; Anna, 36; Bertha, 11, 34; Ernest, 36; Julia, 36; Rosa, 4, 11, 14, 34; Minnie, 10; Walter, 37
Waters, Ortha, 40, 44
Woolery, Inez, 5

ADA BELL GUYTON

Ada Bell came from a long line of Scotch-Irish Bells who settled in Virginia in the 1700's, migrated to Kentucky in the early 1800's, then to Oregon in 1850. Her grandfather, John Robertson Bell, was a lay Methodist preacher who, when he reached Oregon, bought up whiskey stills and dismantled them because he deplored the effects of alcohol on Indians and settlers alike. His son, Josiah Dock, was Ada's father.

Her great-grandfather on her mother's side was Seth Lake who built the first stone hotel in Golden, Colorado— the Astor House—when the Provincial Legislature met there. The hotel has been designated as one of a number of National Historic Landmarks in Golden.

Hulbert, son of Seth Lake, was a rolling stone who seldom lived anyplace more than three or four years. He reached Colorado years before his father, during the Pike's Peak gold rush. He said, "In 1849, I pitched my tent on the plain where the City of Denver now stands."

Eventually he bought land on the Clackamas River near Eagle Creek, Oregon, about the time John R. Bell took a land grant three miles to the north. There Leonora Samantha Josephine Lake met Josiah Dock Bell at a joint school affair. A classmate asked Josie, "Who is that boy writing his name on the blackboard with both hands at once, backward with left hand, forward with right?" Josie answered, "That's Dock Bell, and he thinks he's pretty smart."

Before many months went by Josie, 16, and Dock, 18, were married. Work was scarce and they sought security in one mill town after another; finally Dock took a homestead near Boyd, Oregon. They managed to feed their growing family by both "working out" for neighbors; Dock did field work and Josie housework.

Ada's vivid memory of her childhood was recorded in a diary she kept over 50 years, in a family history, and many other writings. For many years she was the local correspondent for newspapers in Sherman County and The Dalles.

Even during her busy years keeping their farm home and caring for four children, she continued to be a leavening influence for good in her community. When she believed someone needed a friend, she put on her hat and went to call, and became that friend.

She read avidly, choosing reading material that enlarged her understanding. It might be said that she transferred the talents which made her a fine teacher to the home she shared with her husband, Will Guyton, and their family.

THE AUTHOR

One of the first recollections of Helen Guyton is being allowed to look at the keepsakes of her mother Ada Bell Guyton. Who can say how Ada knew when it was exactly the right time to take down from its place on the shelf the box of treasures? Not every day, or month, or year was the time. Somehow it came when her youngest daughter most needed to touch and imagine and believe.

Once the promise had been made to handle things carefully and put them back in order, the censory-stimulating collection of keepsakes was placed on the carpet before her, and an afternoon of wonder and delight unfolded, as she caught the aroma of old paper. First out was the invitation to a party. She touched the pink satin bow in the corner. Then she saw the Christmas bell that opened with crackling paper fluting. Four gold-embossed gift editions of classics could be lifted out long before they could be understood. A small plush book with a metal clasp contained pictures of a long-ago schoolhouse with children lined up before the door, and friends whose names she had heard mentioned.

As soon as she learned to read, Helen read every inspiring printed word and in her innocent childlike mind, agreed that it was all true.

Sadness came over her when she opened the little album and saw the curls clipped from Uncle John's blond head. Her mother had cried when those curls were cut. The riddles captured her imagination and the word-rhythms of the poems instilled a love of language.

When she reached the bundle of letters at the bottom of the box, they reminded her it was time to put away the stuff out of which dreams are made. The looking was completed, but the memory lingered.

Years later the young Ada Bell's life was made visible to her grown daughter Helen when she first opened the box containing Ada's writings. The mother who had seemed so invincible and assured, faded out and the uncertain, shy adolescent she had been, stepped out of the pages. Helen, who had guided and encouraged her own children to maturity, wanted to take the frightened Ada in her arms and comfort her. Then she realized that all the problems so vividly described, had long since been dispelled and Ada had become her own comforter and mentor. Ada had long since run her last race, fought the good fight, and remained faithful to the end. There was much to be learned from the thoughts confided to her diary 70 years earlier. Circumstances had surely changed, but the need to do right was alive and well.

Ada often said, "Someday there will be an author in the family; someone who will have to write in spite of the preoccupations of living." It only took her daughter Helen to get it all together. This book is that gathering together of the threads of Ada's thoughts and writings.